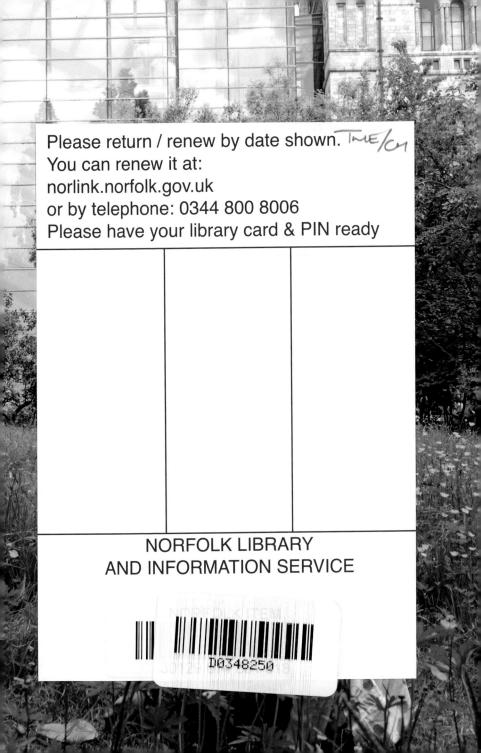

Please return / renew by date shown. TIME/CM
You can renew it at:
norlink.norfolk.gov.uk
or by telephone: 0344 800 8006
Please have your library card & PIN ready

NORFOLK LIBRARY
AND INFORMATION SERVICE

THE wild city book

loads of things to do outdoors in towns and cities

jo schofield and fiona danks

F

FRANCES LINCOLN LIMITED
PUBLISHERS

For Connie, Dan, Edward, Hannah and Jake

Frances Lincoln Ltd
74–77 White Lion Street, London N1 9PF
www.franceslincoln.com
www.goingwild.net

A catalogue record for this book is available from the British
Library.

ISBN 978-0-7112-3488-8

Printed and bound in China

This book contains some potentially dangerous activities.
Please note that any reader or anyone in their charge taking
part in any of the activities described does so at their own
risk. Neither the authors nor the publisher can accept any
legal responsibility for any harm, injury, damage, loss or
prosecution resulting from the use or misuse of the activities,
techniques, tools and advice in the book.
    It is illegal to carry out any of these activities on private
land without the owner's permission, and you should obey
all laws relating to the protection of land, property, plants
and animals.

contents

there's a wild world out there

Do you live in a city? Have you ever spent time outdoors watching wild creatures, climbing trees, making mud pies or hunting for wildlife clues? Believe it or not you don't have to be a brave explorer or travel miles out into the countryside to discover wonderful wildlife, play games in the woods or have exciting outdoor adventures. A wonderful wild world of plants and animals is waiting to be discovered round the corner, right now, in every city; you just need to keep your eyes open and know where to look.

The Wild City Book is all about having fun outdoors in the wild spaces near where you live. You may be surprised by what you find: many cities have more accessible green space than intensively farmed open countryside. This book is packed with ideas for exciting things to make and do in your city's wild corners. You don't have to go to an organised outdoor event; just go outside with your family and friends and use *The Wild City Book* to make your own fun, from imaginary games and creative adventures to wild games and street art.

Wild city adventure bag Every activity in this book is based outdoors. Nature comes conveniently free, so all you need is an adventure bag packed with:

- A copy of this book!
- String, raffia, wool, thin wire and elastic bands

- Masking tape, double-sided sticky tape, PVA glue and scissors
- Old paintbrushes and sponges
- Magnifying glass and bug box
- A basic first aid kit (and make sure someone knows how to use it)
- Clay: educational suppliers and good toyshops sell this at very little cost. Alternatively, try plasticine or this play dough recipe: mix and knead together 1 cup of plain flour, half a cup of salt, 2 tablespoons of cream of tartar, 1 tablespoon of cooking oil and enough water to make a mouldable dough.

Keeping safe in the city

With all the projects in this book, follow the safety guidelines on pages 124 –5. Some activities are easy to try and others are more challenging; remember that what is easy for one person may be tricky for another. The activity code below provides a guide to levels of difficulty and risk, but always take care when playing outdoors, be aware of traffic and stay with friends.

May be possible to do on your own

Some tricky bits which might need a little adult help

Adult supervision essential

1

wildlife in the city

01

discovering wild places in the city

Where can you find wild places in the city? You may play in parks and gardens but there are so many other places to discover. Go outdoors with your family to see if you can find all these wildlife places:

wildlife places

- ☐ an urban nature reserve
- ☐ an urban wood
- ☐ a community garden
- ☐ a city meadow
- ☐ a roof garden
- ☐ an area of common land
- ☐ wild school grounds
- ☐ an urban orchard
- ☐ a churchyard or cemetery
- ☐ a disused railway
- ☐ a cycleway
- ☐ river banks and canal paths
- ☐ a golf course
- ☐ a city farm
- ☐ a botanical garden
- ☐ a reservoir or lake
- ☐ a pond or stream
- ☐ an allotment
- ☐ a green wall or vertical garden
- ☐ a window box

What wildlife can you discover in each place? You might see more creatures if you go out at dawn, dusk or after dark. Look out for large animals such as foxes, bats and birds and also for smaller creatures such as insects and spiders. Can you make a map of the local wild places near where you live, adding pictures of the plants and creatures you found there?

A few tips for discovering and improving city green spaces

The best way to see and protect wildlife is to imagine you are a plant or an animal; what would you need? How would you find shelter and food without being disturbed by

humans or injured by traffic? Help create wildlife 'streets', so plants and animals can move from one green place to another, along rows of trees, hedges, rivers and canals or old railway lines. Make the most of the green spaces you use every day at school, at home, or at the local park. Ask some grown-ups to help you make these places better for wildlife by doing things like letting the grass grow long, making a pile of sticks, planting nectar-rich flowers, native trees and bushes, and not being too neat and tidy!

PROJECT

02 dawn chorus

For a truly magical 'close to nature' experience in the city, go outside on a fine spring or summer morning to discover the dawn chorus. You and your family will need to get up before the sun, wrap in warm clothes, pack a picnic breakfast and then head off to a local wooded green space. As the sun begins to rise you will hear nature's bird orchestra tuning up. If you are wondering how birdsong can compete with the noise of traffic, don't worry: city birds sing louder than country birds! Try recording the dawn chorus on an iPod, saving it as a natural alarm call to wake you up each morning.

mini-beast holiday home

Discover more about amazing creepy-crawlies living in hidden corners of the garden or park.

● Put a layer of damp (but not wet) soil in a plastic container such as a seed tray. Add some bark, dead leaves, a few stones and some vegetable peelings.

● Search under stones and logs in the garden or park for woodlice and other creepy-crawlies; pick them up very gently, perhaps using an old paint brush. Collect the little creatures in a lidded container and then carry them safely to the holiday home. Spray the holiday home with water occasionally. Cover one side of the holiday home to make it dark. Do the little creatures prefer the dark or the light?

After a few days, return the creatures to their natural habitats where you found them. They will be better off out in the big wide world.

04

nature detective scavenger hunt

Many wild animals and birds are hard to spot. They may be secretive, shy or cleverly camouflaged, and some are only active at night. Look for big and small animal clues with your friends. Split into two teams and see which team can take photos of the most clues.

Some clues to look out for:

● Animal restaurants – signs of feeding, such as: nibbled leaves; chewed nuts and fir cones; broken snail shells; piles of feathers; bits of animal skeletons (can you guess what animals they are from?); broken egg shells; scratched or chewed bark on trees.

● Animal highways, such as: the slime trail of a slug or snail; animal footprints; animal pathways through grasses or bushes; ant trails across the surface of the soil.

● Signs of moulting or shedding, such as: loose feathers; insect cases and empty chrysalises; cocoons; tufts of fur.

● Animal homes, such as: birds' nests; ant hills; cuckoo spit (the foam produced by small insects called froghoppers, which lay eggs on grasses); rabbit holes; spiders' webs and nests; molehills; galls.

● Eggs, such as: frogspawn; snail eggs under a stone or log; birds' eggs.

● Animal toilets, such as: wild animal poo; bird droppings; bird pellets (made when birds of prey eject bones and fur in a neat pellet); worm casts (little mounds of worm-processed soil).

Hunting tips
● Don't touch animal waste.
● Don't disturb wildlife or nests.

05

growing food in small spaces

You can grow delicious fruit and vegetables almost anywhere, as long they have light, water, warmth and nutrients. Grow them in containers such as buckets, or plastic or wooden boxes, or painted tin cans. Make a few holes in the bottom of each one so excess water can drain away.

● Choose where to grow your food: perhaps a sheltered corner of the garden, on a balcony, in a shared garden; or, if you don't have much space, you can make a vertical garden up a wall or perhaps grow runner beans up a drainpipe. Some communities grow food together in flower beds, communal gardens and unused land: see www.incredibleediblenetwork.org.uk

Watch in amazement as the dry little seeds grow into beautiful green plants and produce tasty things for you to eat.

● In the spring, buy seeds or young plants of, for example, tomatoes, beans, radishes, runner beans, cut-and-come-again lettuces, strawberries, courgettes.

● Put a few pebbles or bits of broken clay pots in the containers, and then add peat-free compost. Sow seeds or plant out little plants: think how big they will grow and then choose a suitable size of container. Sow each seed to about the same depth as the seed itself. Keep the containers under plastic or on a windowsill indoors until the late spring, when all danger of frost should have passed.

● Check the containers daily in summer: if the compost feels dry to your fingers, add some tap water. Don't over-water – more garden plants die through over-watering than from lack of water.

wildlife service station

Even the smallest outdoor space can provide somewhere for birds, butterflies and other small creatures to take a break and have a meal. Plant out pots, cans and other containers with plants to provide shade, shelter, food and nesting places. When the plants go to seed, leave the seeds for the birds and other wildlife to feast on.

● Choose colourful nectar-rich flowers with a good spread of flowering times so the pots will provide a nectar café from spring right through to the autumn.

● How about a wildlife wall? Ask your neighbours to join in too. Build up layers of pots filled with plants that produce lots of nectar or seeds.

● Group your containers together on a tray or table, up a ladder or on steps, to make watering easier and provide more hidey-holes for wildlife.

● Choose plants that might provide food or flavouring for you too – perhaps herbs such as marjoram, mint, chives and sage; or you could try nasturtiums, sunflowers or lavender.

nectar café

To watch butterflies in summer at very close quarters, place this feeder among flowers growing in a garden or on a balcony.

● Cut the top third off a clear plastic bottle and remove the cap. Cut the sides of the lower two-thirds of the bottle into strips.

● Bend the plastic strips outwards to make a flower shape, covering them with brightly painted cardboard petals. Experiment with different-coloured petals. Which colours do the butterflies like best?

● Place the bottle 'flower' in the inverted bottle neck. Find a straight stick and push it into the ground or a plant pot in a sunny spot. Push the butterfly feeder over the stick. Place a small sponge in the bowl for butterflies to stand on while feeding.

● Wait for a sunny day and then pour dilute sugar solution into the feeder. Who comes to feed?

● Try adding different over-ripe fruits – mushy banana, for example. Which fruits do the butterflies prefer?

08

mini-beast hunting

Pack up a mini-beast hunting kit and go on a mini-expedition to discover little creatures.

DIY mini-beast hunting kit

● A spoon and a small paint brush (for picking up mini-beasts).

● An old sheet (shake the branch of a bush over the sheet; what mini-beasts will appear?).

● A collection of plastic containers; jam jars or clear plastic pots are especially useful for watching mini-beasts.

● A magnifying glass and/or a bug box, so you can get up really close.

● An identification kit such as a simple field guide, or try the Internet (e.g. www.opalexplorenature.org).

Safety tips (for the mini-beasts!)

● Handle mini-beasts as little as possible and always be very gentle.

● Put the mini-beasts back in the same sort of place as you find them.

Where to look and what to look for

● cool, damp places under stones, logs and in shady corners – millipedes, centipedes, beetles, earwigs, woodlice and slugs

● long grass and dead leaves – snails, beetles, spiders

● on trees and bushes – ladybirds, spiders, shield bugs and other bugs and beetles

● in soil – worms, grubs

● on flowers – butterflies, bees and other nectar-seeking insects

09

ready, steady, bioblitz!

Team up with friends and neighbours to find out about the wildlife living in your patch.

A bioblitz brings together scientists, wildlife experts and local people to discover as many wild plants and animals as possible over 24 hours. You could do your own version of a mini-bioblitz in your garden, among the pots on a patio, or in a one-metre square at the park. Try a larger study up and down your street, in the local park or at school.

Use a roll of lining paper to record everything you discover, sticking leaves from different plants on double-sided tape and drawing pictures of animals you spot or find signs of. You will be amazed by how much wildlife you will find in a small town garden. For further information visit www.bnhc.org.uk/home/bioblitz/run-your-own.html. Information on identifying wildlife is on the iSpot website www.ispot.org.

Use a bugbox to see the smallest creatures and tiniest plants.

10 mini-beast mansion

Most of the thousands of mini-beasts in parks and gardens do useful things such as pollinating flowers and recycling rotting leaves and wood. Make mini-beast mansions in the autumn for creepy-crawlies seeking shelter over the winter.

● Choose a good location, perhaps by a fence or wall where it's not too sunny.

● Make the structure from old bricks, tiles or bits of wood; build a base, walls and several floors. Air bricks provide perfect holes for mini-beasts to shelter in.

● Try to copy features found in nature: fill gaps with hollow stems, grasses, bark, leaves, pine cones to provide cosy hiding places. Alternatively, hammer together three bits wood, and fill the hole with hollow stems.

hedgehog homes

Like too many wild creatures, hedgehogs find it hard to seek places to live. Parks and gardens can provide shelter and food (slugs, beetles and worms), but hedgehogs can't climb over big fences. They like to hide in compost heaps and piles of sticks and leaves in quiet corners where they can rummage for grubs. As winter approaches, prepare this snug hibernation shelter, a cosy place to sleep until spring.

● Choose a quiet spot that won't be disturbed, perhaps near a fence or hedge. Make a square base, perhaps with some old bricks. The entrance shouldn't face north or north-east. Cover the bricks with a plastic box or a lid. Add some bedding of dry grass and leaves, shredded newspaper or straw.

● Lean a few sticks over the hedgehog house. Cover them with a thick layer of autumn leaves, building up from the ground.

● Tempt hedgehogs with a little meat-based pet food and a saucer of water. If you think a hedgehog is hibernating, leave it undisturbed until the spring.

12

make a mini-pond

A pond is perhaps the best way to attract wildlife to a garden. Even a mini-pond provides homes for plants and animals and a watering place for birds. A frog was spotted in this mini-pond!

● Find a suitable container – perhaps a dustbin lid, a plastic box, an old sink or a washing-up bowl.

● Choose a quiet place, somewhere sheltered but not totally in the shade. During autumn or winter, bury the container in the ground so the top is level with the surface of the soil. If there is no bare soil place a few bricks, logs and stones around it so creatures such as frogs can get in and out easily.

● Place a little soil and a few stones in the container and then fill it with rainwater and wait for wildlife to arrive in the spring. You may add a few small pond plants, but only use native species.

Safety tip If very small children use your garden, cover the pond with a grill of some sort.

snail settlement

● Put some moist soil into a large clear container. Add some moss, rotting wood, bark, stones, leaves, a small plant or two and some snail food: lettuce, leaves or raw vegetable peelings.

● Go out after it's rained to collect a few snails; look under plants and stones. Place them gently in the jar and then fix some kitchen roll over the opening. Snails like fresh food and a well-ventilated, clean, damp environment.

● Watch how the snails behave, what they eat and where they like to go. If they feel really at home they may lay eggs, so look out for baby snails developing.

● After a couple of weeks or so, return the snails to where you found them.

early bird buffet

Many birds struggle to find enough food over the winter, but you can help by making these simple feeders. Ask a grown-up to hang them above a window and small birds will soon be feeding just the other side of the glass.

Fir-cone feeders Collect some cones and place them somewhere warm so they open out fully. Smear softened lard between the cone's bracts. Pour some mixed birdseed on to a plate. Spread the seeds over the lard. Tie some string around the top or bottom of the cone and hang it up in a tree or above a window.

Twig feeder Find a branched twig with rough bark. Coat it with lard, then cover with birdseed.

Willow-ring feeder Weave a ring of bendy willow and push a stick through one side of it to make a perch. Push a skewer through the willow into the middle of the ring. Thread fruit on to the skewer before pushing it through the other side of the ring.

A fir-cone treat for a hungry blue tit.

recycled bird feeders

Rummage through the recycling bin to find things to make into bird feeders.

Wire feeder Wind some thick wire round a broom handle, a can or any smooth cylinder to make a spiral. Thread dried or fresh fruit along the spiral.

Tin can feeder Paint a metal food can as you wish, using acrylic paint. With help from a grown-up, make a hole in the tin's base with a bradawl, and then poke a stick right through it. Attach a bit of wood over the end to stop the seeds or nuts from falling out.

Plastic feeder bottles Tie some string below the lid of a small plastic bottle so you can hang it up, and poke little holes in the bottom of the bottle so water can drain away. Then cut a panel out of one side of the bottle and pour in peanuts. Or, alternatively, push wooden spoons through the bottle at right angles to each other, make a small hole above the bowl of each spoon and fill the bottle with birdseed.

Carton feeder Decorate a milk or juice carton with waterproof acrylic paint. Cut a couple of doors in it and make a stick perch. Fill with peanuts and hang it up.

Don't forget to top up the feeders regularly until the spring, when more natural food is available.

2

wild creations

16

grass seed heads

During late summer, find some long grass in the park or a wild green space. How many different grasses can you spot? Collect grass seed heads in a plastic bag, and then make a funny character with a wild hair-do.

● Cut one leg off a pair of tights, stretch the toe over a jam jar and then pour in some grass seeds. Put moist soil or peat-free compost on top of the seeds to make a ball, making sure the grass seeds are spread out. Tie a knot in the tights to secure the soil in place. Pour water into the jar and then place the ball on the rim, making sure the seeds are on the top. The end of the tights should hang down into the water.

● Place on a windowsill and wait for the grass to grow. Add more water when necessary.

● Once the grass hair has grown, attach natural features and decorate the jar to make a funny character. You will be able to cut its hair, and the grass will grow back again and again, as long as you remember to water it.

17 hairy herbs

Transform homemade plant pots into these funny little characters with edible hair.

● Cut long strips (about 60 cm/2ft long by 10cm/4in wide) of several sheets of newspaper or brown paper. Wrap the paper strips around a straight-sided jar, a tin can or a glass, with about 2.5cm/1in of paper protruding beyond the container's open

end. Tuck the loose paper into the opening to make a base and then slide the pot off the container, flattening the base if need be. Alternatively, you can make a cardboard pot from a toilet-roll holder: cut slits in one end and then push the flaps in to make the base.

● Fill your pot with soil or peat-free compost. Sow with herb seeds (perhaps chives or parsley) or plant herbs as small plants. Bring your pot to life with natural features such as seedy eyes, a twiggy nose and a leafy mouth stuck on with PVA glue or pushed into small holes in the pots. Place the pots on a tray on a windowsill. Remember to water them!

18

flower chains

Long, hot, lazy summer days in the park are perfect for lounging on the grass and making flower chains. Pick daisies or dandelions with long stems. Use your thumbnail (best if you have quite a long nail!) to make a small split in the end of a stem so you can thread another stem through it. Keep adding more flowers in the same way.

● How many daisies tall are you? Or how many dandelions? Try the daisy chain challenge – who can make the longest chain?

● Can you make flower chains into crowns, necklaces, earrings, bracelets or festive bunting? Alternatively, try threading fallen flowers or petals on to wool or string to make garlands.

Flower chain tips

Flower chains may keep for longer if you dry them in an airing cupboard. Only make chains from flowers that are very common.

Thread fallen flowers or petals on to wool or string to make garlands.

19

wild pictures

Collect a few loose natural materials from a favourite wild place. Can you use them to create a wonderful wild picture?

● Find a piece of stiff card, about A5 size. You will need PVA glue or double-sided sticky tape. The tape is easier to use but you will need to cover one side of the card completely with tape.

● Make a frame around the edge of the card. It might be a plain frame of grasses or long leaves, or you may prefer to design a more complicated pattern.

● Now design a picture. Double-sided tape is pretty sticky and you won't be able to move things around, so you might like to mock up the picture first.

leafy book covers

Use autumn leaves to design a special cover for a treasured sketchbook or notebook.

● This works best on a book with a stiff rough-textured cover. Go to a park or garden to hunt for coloured leaves. Choose thin, soft leaves without thick veins, as they will bend easily around a book's spine.

● Paint slightly diluted PVA glue over one side of the cover. Starting in one corner, arrange leaves over the glue, layering them over each other. Paint more PVA on top of the leaves as you add them. Keep working across the cover until one side is completely decorated, pasting the leaves over and around the edges for a smooth finish.

● Let the glue dry and then repeat on the other side and down the spine. For a smoother, stronger finish, paint the whole cover with at least one more coat of diluted PVA.

21 leaf bowls and plates

- Collect dry, colourful leaves and press them between layers of newspaper for a couple of days. Choose some plastic plates and bowls: you will need two of each so you can sandwich leaves between them.

- Cover the outside of a bowl or plate in cling film. Arrange layers of leaves over the cling film, pasting them together with slightly diluted PVA glue.

- Once you have glued several layers of leaves together over the outside of the plate or bowl, lay another piece of cling film over the top, and then put a matching plate or bowl over the top to sandwich everything together. Let the glue dry over a few days and then carefully remove the outer bowl or plates and the cling film. Paint diluted PVA over the exposed leaves. Let it dry, remove the other bowl and then paint PVA over the other surface.

trick pictures

Can you play tricks on your friends by taking funny photographs that fool the eye by making the big look small and the small look big? Take the photos on a bright sunny day to get the right depth of field, or they won't look so convincing.

23

land art in the park

Have a new look at your local park. Can you use some of its natural treasures to create wild art? Or maybe transform the park furniture into an imaginary creature?

Ephemeral natural pictures Look for loose natural materials such as sticks, leaves and pinecones. Find a patch of grass and make a

collage of a bird, a dragon, a monster or whatever the materials inspire.

Make arty shadows This park bench has been disguised as a crazy shadow horse with just a bucket, a plastic bottle, a sponge and a few sticks. What weird shadow creatures can you make?

Daisy and dandelion pictures At first glance you might see a lawn covered in daisies, but can you spot the face hiding among them?

24

blackberry treats

Autumn is blackberry time; look for them beside old railway lines, rivers and canals, in churchyards and at allotments.

Blackberry smoothie Put a handful of blackberries in a blender with some natural yoghurt and a little honey; press the button to blend into a lovely purple smoothie.

Blackberry muffins Mix together 1 egg, 40g caster sugar, 50g melted butter, 110ml of milk and half a teaspoon of vanilla extract. Mix in 150g of self-raising flour and add 100g of freshly picked blackberries. Spoon the mixture into prepared muffin trays. Cook for about 20 minutes at 200°C/220°F/gas mark 5. Enjoy!

Safety tip Make sure an adult helps you to identify blackberries, and don't collect them from roadsides.

snow people

Try a different take on your average snowman by making realistic snow figures in unusual places. How about a lady sitting on a bench, an old man waiting at the bus stop, a child on a swing in the playground or someone leaning against a tree trunk in the park?

snowball mobiles

Go outside on a white wintry day and collect a bag or a box of snow to take home ready to make a mobile to hang in the garden or outside a window.

● You will also need several short sticks (about 5cm/2in); tie each one on to a length of string or wool. Shape a snowball around each little stick.

● Now for the fun part! Use natural materials to transform the snowballs into birds, rabbits, monsters, or maybe some pretty baubles.

Hang the decorated snowballs from sticks and enjoy your wintry mobile until the temperature rises and the snow melts.

27

snow buildings

Rush outside after a fresh fall of snow and become an architect and builder.

● You will need plastic containers in different shapes and sizes, a flat plastic spade, and an old knife and spoon to shape the snow.

● How many different buildings can you make? Build a little cottage, a magical castle with turrets, a towering factory with rows of tall chimneys, or huge skyscrapers and highways for your toy cars.

● Or take inspiration from buildings in your city, like this little snow church.

● Photograph your architectural masterpieces before they melt!

3

imaginative play

PROJECT

28 teddy bears' picnic

Take your teddies for an outing to the garden, the park or a wild green space. Make them a shelter and arrange a picnic with natural cups and plates and wild foods you have gathered. They might drink dew from the early morning grass with a feast of daisy hearts and dandelion leaves, or sip tea from an acorn cup or a walnut shell.

make a mini-igloo

How would your teddy like a snowy adventure? Perhaps you could make an igloo village so your friends' teddies can join in too!

● Wrap up for the cold and put on warm waterproof gloves.

● Push snow into a small rectangular container, level the top and then tip out a perfect little brick.

● Decide how big your teddy's igloo should be. Place snow bricks in a circle, leaving a suitable-sized gap for an entrance. Arrange a second layer of bricks over the first, taking care to cover the gaps between the bricks in the first layer and placing the second layer slightly nearer the centre of the circle.

● Keep adding layers in this way until the walls meet at the top.

After dark, you can replace each teddy with a night light and ask an adult to light them; enjoy the magical glow-in-the-dark mini-igloos.

grass dolls

These natural dolls are made from long grasses collected from uncut areas.

● Hold a bunch of long grasses in your hand, binding them together roughly in the middle: this will be the doll's body. Do the binding with other flexible grasses, long thin leaves, or with wool, thread or raffia.

● Separate the lower part of the bunch of grass into two bunches to make the legs. Bind these down to the end, bending the bottom bit at an angle to make feet.

● Take another thinner bunch of slightly shorter grass stems. Push this through the body of the doll to make arms. Bind the arms and make hands at the ends.

● For the head, bind the grasses above where the arms are, leaving the ends loose as a crazy hair style if you like. Stick on natural materials such as berries and seeds to make features, or alternatively draw a face on a leaf and stick this on to the head.

natural fashions

These cardboard dolls will love wearing the latest natural fashions or being transformed into fairies or princesses.

● Draw and paint a doll and a base on stiff card; cut it out, and cut two vertical slits up from the bottom of the base. Cut two small card rectangles to push through the slits as shown, so the doll can stand up. You will need some small Velcro sticky pads; stick the hooked pads on the doll's body, wrists and head and feet. Cut the pads to a smaller size if necessary.

● Go outside and search for beautiful natural materials such as seeds, coloured leaves, petals and feathers. Design some clothes, cutting leaves into different shapes and sticking them together with double-sided tape if need be. Stick small pieces of soft loop Velcro onto the back of the outfit to match the hook pads on the doll's body, and dress the doll.

● Try designing seasonal fashion collections; perhaps grass skirts in summer, bright leafy outfits in autumn and evergreen leaves in winter. Some outfits won't last long but the dolls will be very happy to have new dresses for every party!

conker and pine cone creatures

Make funny creatures and characters from large tree seeds such as conkers, sweet chestnuts and fir cones.

Conker characters Choose some big conkers. Use a bradawl or skewer to make holes in the conkers. (You will need help from an adult.) Use thin twigs or matchsticks to join conkers together and to make arms and legs. Add leaves and other natural materials to make hair, hats and any other features you need to bring your character to life.

Cone creatures Use little bits of clay or plasticine as glue to stick on legs and other details, perhaps like this fir cone cat with its twig legs, berry nose and pine needle whiskers.

Ask a grown-up to help you use a bradawl or skewer to make holes in the conkers.

nature's kitchen

The perfect place for free messy play and stirring up wonderful mud pies, cakes, soups and stews. The dish in this frying pan started as bark bacon and a dandelion egg but ended up as Digby's special pancake delight!

● Choose a quiet, untidy corner of the garden where it's fine to make a mess and have fun, perhaps against a wall or a fence. Make sure there's some mud nearby, as this is an essential ingredient. Ask a grown-up to help build a kitchen with wood, bricks and boxes; an old shelf propped up on bricks makes a good worktop.

● Add a cardboard cooker, a cardboard cupboard and perhaps some little chairs and a table if you want to have a party: the design is entirely up to you.

● Fill your kitchen with old pots, pans and cutlery. Empty milk and juice cartons and other everyday objects are perfect for pretend play.

● Additional useful ingredients include stones, sand, sticks, water and perhaps leaves and a few petals. Have fun!

4 celebrations

& festivals

34

natural fireworks

Scared of noisy fireworks? These silent natural fireworks twist and turn in the breeze, a perfect decoration for a bonfire party.

Wind twizzlers Gather brightly coloured autumn leaves; press them in a large heavy book if you aren't using them right away. Draw a spiral on one side of a stiff paper plate. Use PVA glue to stick leaves on the other side of the plate. Paint more glue over the leaves; it will go clear and shiny, bringing out the natural colours. Cut the plate along the line of the spiral. Poke a hole in the very centre. Tie a large knot in the end of some string or wool and push it through the hole. Hang your twizzler outside and twist the string to make it spin around.

Fireballs Tie string tightly around a short stick. Make a ball of clay around the stick and hang it up ready to decorate. Cut some straight thin red, green and brown sticks to about 30cm/12in. Thread colourful leaves along each stick, and then push the sticks into the clay to make a dramatic fireball.

35

leaf decorations

Leaf bunting

Hang this autumn leaf bunting up on a balcony, around a garden terrace or outside a window to decorate an outdoor harvest festival, a Halloween celebration or a bonfire party. Thread a long piece of wool on to a large needle, such as a sail needle. Sew the wool through the coloured leaves in a running stitch. For added contrast, sew different coloured leaves on top of each other.

Leaf chains

These leaf chains are made in the same way as daisy chains. Place a leaf with a long stalk on a hard surface such as a chopping board. Roll the stalk as flat as you can with a rolling pin or perhaps a pencil or a biro. Make a split near the end of a flattened stalk using the pointed end of a biro or a cocktail stick. Repeat with more long-stalked leaves. Thread the leaves together in a long chain by pushing the stalks through the splits.

71

36

shiny leaves for winter

A great way to brighten up the barest winter tree.

● Collect autumn leaves with interesting shapes and strong vein patterns. Look for some foil: aluminium cooking foil, coloured foil from sweet wrappers, or the thick foil tops from tubs of margarine, butter or yoghurt.

● Place some foil over a leaf. Hold in place with one finger where the stalk joins the leaf. Rub the foil firmly with the fingers of your other hand: try to pick up all the veins and the outline of the leaf.

● Cut out each shiny leaf and thread cotton or fine wire through each one. Hang them on a tree outside or bring some winter twigs indoors to decorate.

leafy lanterns

Add some magic to a party with these pretty lanterns. Try summer petals, autumn leaves, or winter leaf skeletons and evergreen leaves.

● Find some glass jars or clear plastic yoghurt pots. Tie some string tightly around the top of each one to make handles.

● Use elastic bands to hold leaves or other materials in place. Overlap the leaves for best effect. You may wish to cut patterns or faces in the leaves before you put them on the jar.

● Place a night light in each jar. Hang the lanterns outside on a tree or balcony, or stand them on a windowsill.

Safety tip Only use night lights when with an adult.

natural halloween

Have a fun-filled, creepy, natural Halloween!

Clay and pine cone bats Tie string around a very short stick. Wrap clay around the stick and mould into an oval shape to make the bat's body. Alternatively, use a pine cone as the body and stick on the details using clay. Add leafy wings and big ears, little beady eyes and a big mouth.

Witch's or wizard's hat Decorate a black card hat with pumpkin faces cut out of orange autumn leaves, sticking them on with double sided tape or glue.

Leaf bats Collect batwing-shaped sycamore, maple or plane leaves. Cut a bat head with long ears at the stalk end of each leaf. Thread leaf bats along wool to make batty bunting.

Pumpkin monsters Spoon the flesh and seeds out of a pumpkin and then ask an adult to help carve features. Add natural details such as twiggy horns, berry eyes and a red leaf tongue.

Special spiders Make a clay body (see bat above) or use a fir cone. Press clay in the underside of the cone, and then push in 8 thin twigs or stems to make legs. Stick some seeds or little pebbles onto the cone with clay to make big eyes.

39 ice bunting

When the world sparkles with cold, this ice bunting provides unusual window dressing or a garden decoration. How long will the bunting last? How do the icy shapes change as the weather freezes and thaws?

● Find a few cookie cutters and some shallow plastic boxes or metal baking trays.

● Collect some leaves and seeds; even in the depths of winter you can find special natural treasures. Go outside and pour water into each container to a depth of about 1cm/½ inch. Add a few drops of food colouring if you like. Place pastry cutters in some of the baking trays. Arrange a few natural treasures in each shape.

● Cut some lengths of thin wire, twisting one end of each length. Place a wire in each shape, with the twisted end in the water and the other end hanging over the edge.

● Leave to freeze overnight, and then use some warm water to remove the ice from the containers. Tie a line of string outside a window, in a tree or along a balcony. Use the wire to hang the ice bunting along the string; perfect for a wintry party!

Leave the containers outside overnight to freeze.

40

tree dressing

Do you have a favourite tree? Maybe you enjoy it for climbing and hiding, but it will also be special as a wildlife home, as a source of wood, and because its leaves help to clean the city's air.

Try decorating trees or winter branches with natural and recycled decorations for Christmas or other winter occasions. Or join in with Tree Dressing Day in early December to celebrate the importance of trees in our lives. Here are a few suggestions for dressing a special tree:

● Hang foil leaves (see page 72) or leafy lanterns (see page 73) from the branches.

● Hang some special bird feeders (see page 30) in the tree.

● Make leaf decorations (see page 70). If the weather is really cold, try some ice bunting (see page 76) or ice baubles. Or try making decorations only using what natural materials you can find. Take photographs of your dressed tree; post them on the Going Wild website – www.goingwild.net.

Safety tips (mostly for the tree) Take care not to damage the tree in any way. Don't use nails or anything that might interfere with its growth. You may need to get permission to dress a tree. Never leave lanterns unattended.

chinese dragon

Celebrate Chinese New Year with a dragon costume.

● Cut a long thin triangle from an old sheet (this one is about 2m/6ft long).

● Collect sticks and leaves. With adult help, use hot glue to stick leaves along one edge of the triangle to make spines. Use more leaves to make scales. Attach 4 straight sticks at intervals along the body and tail.

● For the head, make a mask frame to fit your head. Stick two more cardboard strips on as shown to make the upper and lower jaw; you will be looking out of the jaws when you wear it. Give your dragon big scary eyes and a huge mouth full of teeth; this one has pine cone eyes, stick teeth and nut shell nostrils.

● Attach the body to the back of the head with hot glue or double-sided tape. Wear the costume and ask friends to hold the sticks to support the tail; can you move together and do a dragon dance?

5 storytelling

& music

42

wild wind chimes

The tinkling of natural wind chimes hanging in a tree or on a balcony may remind you of outdoor adventures.

● Go on a scavenger hunt to find natural objects that will make a noise if they bang together. You will also need a freshly cut bendy stick, preferably hazel or willow.

● Find a metal lid without sharp edges, e.g. from a syrup or treacle can. Ask an adult to help you make a small hole in the centre of the lid with a sharp bradawl.

● Weave a willow ring just a bit larger than the metal lid (see page 31). Push a stick across the middle of the willow ring.

Tie a big knot in one end of a 20cm/8in length of wool. Thread it through the lid and attach to the stick on your willow circle.

Hang sticks and other natural materials from the willow ring using wool; each item should be close enough to the metal lid to hit it when the wind blows.

tin can busking

Bash the swinging xylophone with a big stick to see how many different sounds you can make. This noisy activity is perfect for the park.

● Collect tin cans of different sizes, some big sticks and perhaps some plastic bottles part-filled with pebbles or dried beans.

● Ask a grown-up to use a bradawl to make holes in the bottom of each can. Now thread the cans along some string, decorating with a few fir cones or other natural materials if you wish.

● Go to the park and find a place to hang up your strings of cans and any other noisy things you have found. Play your crazy hanging xylophone; how much noise can you make? (Try to be tuneful so as not to upset the neighbours!) See *The Stick Book* for tin can guitars and more ideas on natural music-making.

miniature wildlife world

Do you think you could make an imaginary habitat full of miniature wildlife? It must have a sun, plants, animals which eat plants and animals which eat animals, and also places for animals to find shelter or make nests.

● To make a miniature wildlife world you will need a shoe box or a seed tray with a thin layer of soil, sand or peat-free compost.

● Collect natural treasures, such as twigs, leaves, moss, seeds and little stones. Transform your finds into miniature trees and plants, and combine them with clay or play dough to make tiny creatures. Don't forget to add the sun, the essential ingredient supporting life on earth.

● You may like to copy a real wildlife habitat or to invent an imaginary one. When your mini-world is complete, perhaps you could make up a story about an explorer discovering everything that lives there.

45 clay gargoyles

Go on a hunt in your city to discover and photograph the faces of gargoyle monsters, animal door knockers and sculptures of creatures.

● Take some clay to the park or a garden and look for places with rough surfaces to make funny clay faces, e.g., walls, fences or tree trunks.

● Mould a lump of clay into a flattish shape and stick it in your chosen spot. Using the faces you photographed earlier as inspiration, try to mould your own gargoyles and monsters, using natural materials to add details if you wish.

● How many faces can your friends spot hidden round the garden or at the park? Can you make up a story trail?

● Leave the faces for a while for others to spot and enjoy, but remove them after a week or so.

snow gargoyles

How many different snow faces and monsters can you make? Here are a few ideas:

Scary skull Start with a big snowball and see what faces you can cut and carve.

Snow monsters Look for unusual places to make funny snow monsters, like this snow gremlin made on a garden chair.

Sunny faces Mould the snow into a sun and make a face.

Cargoyles Transform a snow-covered car into a cargoyle by scraping the snow into ugly or funny faces.

sock puppets

Those worn-out odd socks at the bottom of the drawer may come in handy after all!

● Stuff a sock with scrunched-up newspaper to keep it rigid while you bring it to life. Decide what creature you will make; maybe a wild animal you have spotted in the park or an invented magical beast.

● Choose some leaves, seeds and other natural materials to make into eyes, ears and a nose. Ask an adult to help you stick features on with a hot glue gun, or use double-sided tape. Add

whatever details your creature needs, such as antlers or a mane. Don't decorate the sock's toe too much: you will need to move it with your fingers to make an expressive mouth.

● Once the glue has set, remove the newspaper and place the sock over your hand. Turn the toe in around your fingers to make the mouth. Perhaps you could put on a sock puppet play with your friends.

● To find out about making hobby creatures from an old sock and a stick, see our book *Run Wild*.

Safety tip Hot glue guns should only be used under close supervision.

flying creatures

Birds, butterflies, bees, moths and dragonflies are just some of the flying creatures you might see living in city parks, gardens and other green spaces. Some may be really tiny, so keep your eyes peeled. After dark on summer evenings you may even see bats feeding on moths attracted by streetlights. Have a go at making real or imagined flying creatures.

● Look for a stick that could be made into a flying creature. If you want your creature to hang in a tree or outside your window, tie string, wool or raffia on to the stick at two points to make a loop, or make a handle with another stick.

● Bring your stick to life by wrapping clay or play dough around it to make a body and a head. Attach leaves and other natural bits and pieces to make wings, a tail, eyes and whatever other details your creature needs.

Hang your creatures up or use them as puppets in a show.

49

wild masks

Make eye masks or full face masks from old cereal boxes. Use glue or double-sided tape to stick leaves and other natural materials on the masks, transforming them into real or imaginary city animals, like this fox with red autumn leaves and bird with leafy beak and feathers.

● To hold the eye masks in place, tape a straight stick on the back at one side.

● To attach the full face masks, make a cardboard frame to fit your head as follows: cut two lengths of cardboard about 5cm/2in wide by 30cm/1ft long. Fix them together in a cross. Cut another length about 5cm/2in wide by 60cm/2ft long. Bend this round to fit your head and fix the ends together. Tape the cross of card over the circle and tape to the mask.

Leaf masks Decorate the biggest, toughest leaves you can find with bits of coloured leaf stuck on with double-sided tape. Cut out eyeholes and then tape a stick down the centre of the mask to stiffen it and hold it in place.

stick totem poles

Native American totem poles carved with animals, plants, humans and mythical creatures symbolize a deep respect for the natural world. A totem is an object representing an animal or plant believed to have spiritual significance. What plant or animal is most special to you?

● Choose a long strong knobbly stick with rough bark. Push the stick firmly into the ground or into a pot of soil. Wrap lumps of clay around the stick, perhaps at the most knobbly points so they won't slip down.

● Create totem pole characters by moulding each lump of clay into an animal, a plant or a mythical character, adding details with natural materials. Perhaps you could make a food chain with the sun, plants, a rabbit and a bird of prey, or you may wish to invent imaginary characters for a wild story.

Stick totem poles are a fun way to illustrate natural food chains and tell stories.

51

snowtem poles

● To make snowy versions of totem poles, use large plastic containers to make snow bricks, tapping the snow down with your hands before tipping it out, rather like making a sandcastle.

● Build up a tower, snow block on top of snow block. How high can you make it? Push a little snow between the bricks to join them together.

● Use a spoon or trowel to carve animal features. Add evergreen leaves for wings or ears, berries for eyes or noses – whatever you need to bring it to life!

● If there's only a light dusting of snow, stack up little snowballs to make miniature snowtem poles.

Can you make up a fantastical story about your snowtem pole creatures?

6

wild streets

street games and obstacle courses

Adapt or invent games to play on the pavement, on a hard playground at the park or at school, or in the street, but only when it's safe to do so. What can you play with a few sticks and some chalk, or using street or park furniture?

● Noughts and crosses with sticks, stones or flowers.

● Try sticky hopscotch. Throw a stone into a square, hop along to it and try to pick it up without wobbling any of the sticks.

● Who needs play equipment? Make up your own obstacle courses, a simple, easy version of Parkour, using whatever is in the environment to move yourself through a space. Compete with friends to do a timed course, perhaps jumping on to bollards and somersaulting round metal bars.

● How about a game with nothing but the pavement? Anyone stepping on the cracks between the paving stones is out; the last player left in wins the game. Or maybe anyone stepping on a crack has to carry out a silly forfeit.

Safety tip Stay safe and only play these games in a traffic-free space.

53 close the street

Would you like the chance to play safely and freely with your friends in your street? Just ask the adults to work together to organize a special street play session by closing the street to all traffic for a couple of hours.

Playing out in the street may be the first step to discovering your local area. In your street you might find places to explore, to climb, and to make your own imaginary worlds in front gardens, or within an area outside your house marked by a chalk boundary. Take a toy outside and make a den for it, or take it on some outdoor adventures. For advice and tips on how to start street play sessions, see www.playingout.net.

chalk pictures

Have fun drawing wild pictures, recording wildlife spotted at the park or creating an imaginary wild world.

● You will need some large coloured chalks, available from good toy shops. Draw a background scene on the pavement or at the playground, perhaps with trees, some buildings and a pond or a river. Fill your wild city world with pictures of wild animals and plants you might find nearby. You could draw pictures of mini-beasts you have seen in the city, or fill one paving slab with a picture of an invented wildlife world.

● Draw chalk frames in several paving slabs and fill each one with a picture to make a picture patchwork.

● Take a photo of your finished pictures – you may need to wash them away before you leave.

The picture shown here has an owl, molehills over the hill top and a fox and a hedgehog running over the grass.

water graffiti

Imagine painting outdoors anywhere you want to, and not being told off! Water graffiti only work in dry weather, but on hot sunny days they dry almost as quickly as you can paint them, so work quickly and then take photographs.

● Go outside with buckets of water, some sponges, paintbrushes of different sizes, a paint roller, a spray bottle and anything else that might spread water over a surface.

● Paint, spray and roll water on to walls, pavements and any other surface you can find. Make sure you use plenty of water so your masterpieces can be clearly seen and will survive long enough for you to capture in a photograph.

● And then your graffiti will disappear from sight as if they never existed.

shadow dressing

Can your friends transform your shadow into a crazy monster or a wild princess? This is a great game to play with a group of friends on a sunny day.

● One or two people make shadows on the pavement and the others raid the dressing-up box and hunt for anything that might make details like jewellery, crowns, hair, sunglasses, a fan or a bunch of flowers.

● Take a few stuffed toys outside and dress up their shadows. Can you transform a friendly cuddly toy into a scary shadow monster?

● Try making shadows at different times of day; when the sun is overhead at midday the shadows are rather round with short legs, but in late afternoon the low sunlight casts wonderful long shadows like skinny giants. Take photos of the dressed-up shadows to show your friends.

Use things like jewellery, leaves and sunglasses to dress up your shadow.

57 pavement storyboards

Do you think it might be possible to tell a story with a few sticks and loose natural materials? This game is rather like charades; each team makes a storyboard to illustrate a well-known story or perhaps a nursery rhyme, a song or a book title. The other teams try to guess what stories the pictures are telling.

● Find some sticks to make a series of frames on the pavement or playground, making as many frames as you need to tell your story.

● Collect loose natural materials and create a series of two- or three-dimensional pictures to tell a story, illustrating your favourite book, film, rhyme or song. This storyboard illustrates Little Red Riding Hood. Can you spot the wolf?

spray stencils

These work on any hard surface but they don't last long – so have a camera at the ready.

● Look for materials with interesting shapes– leaves, twigs, things from the recycling box. Cut out cardboard stencils to make houses or castles, tower blocks or bridges, cars or aeroplanes. You might also like to try some non-natural materials that could make effective stencils, such as old CDs.

● Make pictures or patterns using the prepared stencils and collected materials on a patio, a pavement or the school playground. Spray water all around the stencils, then pick them up to reveal a silhouette picture. Can anyone guess what it is or what you used to make it? Try doing a huge picture with your friends.

● What stencil pictures can you make using your hands or feet? Perhaps a tree, an animal or a bird? Or you can lie down and ask a friend to spray water all the way round you to make a full body stencil.

7

games & trails

59 urban elves

Who says that fairies and elves only live at the bottom of pretty country gardens? Perhaps they also hide in the city, living in secret places, watching us as we go about our daily lives. What elf would be able to resist a wonderful home, somewhere to shelter from the rain, lie in a soft feather bed or perhaps eat a meal of gathered nuts or berries?

This secret elf home is made from collected materials, things found in the recycling bin, borrowed from the house or discovered in natural places. Have a go at making a secret elf home, hidden away from the grown-ups!

conkers

Autumn's fallen conkers are collected, counted, rolled like marbles and used in the traditional conker game.

● Play with them as they are, or make them harder by soaking them in vinegar for two minutes and then asking an adult to put them in a very hot oven for two minutes. Let them cool down completely. Ask an adult to poke a hole through each conker with a bradawl or a skewer. Tie a knot in one end of a shoelace; thread the lace through a conker.

● Challenge a friend to a game. Wrap the lace around your hand and then hold the conker out at arm's length hanging down. The other player wraps their lace around their hand and tries to hit your conker with theirs. Take it in turns to hit each other's conkers; the first conker to be destroyed is the loser.

Safety tips Always hold the conkers at arm's length and watch out for bruised knuckles. Don't let any spectators stand too close.

Choose even-shaped conkers that are uncracked and firm.

61 make a parachute man

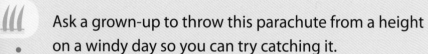

Ask a grown-up to throw this parachute from a height on a windy day so you can try catching it.

● Make a little twig man by tying some sticks together, or weave a grass man (see page 59). To make a parachute, place a plain plastic bag flat on a surface. Fold it in half, and fold in half again. Finally, fold in half diagonally so you end up with a triangular shape. Finish the triangle by cutting off the untidy end to make a straight edge. Open the triangle out to reveal an octagon shape (with eight equal sides).

● Cut 8 pieces of string to about 30cm/1ft. Hold them together in a neat bunch and tie in a knot at one end. Tape the other end of each string to one point on the octagonal parachute as shown. Tie your twig or grass man on to the knotted strings. Take him outside for some parachute adventures!

Safety tip It's safest if adults do the throwing and children do the catching.

sandpit treasure hunts

A sandpit isn't just for digging – it's a great place for treasure hunts and creating imaginary worlds.

Hide natural objects in the sandpit Who can find the most pebbles, shells and seeds hidden in the sand?

Twiggy treasure hunt Hide a few things in the sandpit and stick a twig in the sand above each one. Add lots more twigs with no treasure underneath. Take turns to pull the twigs out, replacing them each time to confuse the other players. You can give points for each piece of treasure, e.g. one for a snail shell, two for a fir cone and three for a pebble.

3-D treasure map game Use natural materials to make a three-dimensional map of your garden in the sandpit. Hide some treasure in the real garden and use a twig cross in the sandpit garden to mark where the treasure is hidden. Can your friends find the real treasure by using the sandpit garden as a treasure map?

Sand worlds Decorate a castle or make an imaginary world using natural materials for the details.

63

paddling pool games

Get the paddling pool out and have fun sending natural boats for scary rides down water chutes.

Testing boats Make boats out of natural materials and test them in the paddling pool to see if they sink or float. Try writing a message on a leaf with a permanent marker and launching it on a river or canal. Perhaps someone will find it! How far did it go?

Water chutes Find or buy some lengths of drainpipe to use as channels. Place chairs near the paddling pool and arrange the drainpipes to make water chutes into the pool. Set a hosepipe to pour water down the chutes. Make little boats and see if they can float down the course into the paddling pool. Try racing two boats at a time – whose boat will win?

Safety tips Children should never play near water unless an adult is with them. Be particularly careful near rivers, canals and ponds.

64 wild croquet

Croquet involves hitting small balls around a course of hoops on a flat grass lawn. Try making your own croquet set with a few sticks.

● Cut six bendy willow or hazel sticks at least 60cm/2ft long and push them in the ground to make hoops, one in each corner of a large rectangle on the grass.

● Paint stripes on a larger stick and put it in the centre of the rectangle. Make another hoop each side of the central post. Or be inventive and make up your own croquet course!

● Each person chooses and paints a stick to use as a mallet, and finds a small ball. Each person takes it in turns to hit their ball with their mallet. The winner is the first person to hit their ball on to the central post, through each hoop and then on to the central post again to finish.

● You can use your ball to hit other people's balls out of the way.

park games

What games can you make up at the park? Here are a few ideas to use as a starting point.

Loop ball Find several bendy sticks (willow or hazel is best) and make a loop at one end of each stick. Push the sticks into the ground to make a course. The aim is to throw a small ball through each loop in the course.

Bottle skittles Find some big plastic bottles and fill them with water, adding a few drops of food colouring. Stand the filled bottles in a line and take it in turns to try and knock them over by throwing a ball at them.

Ring sticks Weave some bendy willow into a circle to make your own ring frisbee. Each person has a stick and someone throws the ring randomly to one of them. If someone doesn't catch the ring on their stick they must go down on one knee; miss again and it's a silly forfeit.

66

ice games

On a freezing cold day, look through ice windows, jump on icy puddles or throw ice pieces over frozen puddles and watch them shatter. Or pretend to be an archaeologist excavating treasures from the ice.

● Put some plastic animals or dinosaurs, or natural materials, in plastic pots or a washing up bowl full of water. Leave outside on a freezing cold night. If it's summer, put them in the freezer instead. Remove the ice blocks from the containers, using a little warm water if need be.

● Have fun bashing, scraping and melting the ice, using warm water, and a selection of tools such as fork and spoon, a stick and a hammer.

● Once you have found the treasures, make sculptures or pictures with the broken ice.

Safety tips Take care when using a hammer. Always wear gloves when handling ice.

techno trails

Smart phones and other hand-held devices can be used for outdoor adventures. Here are a couple of examples.

Geo-caching High-tech treasure hunts which use GPS-enabled mobile devices to find weatherproof treasure boxes hidden in secret places. This global game is played in both country and city; see www.geocaching.com. Make up your own local version: ask some grown-ups to lay a trail in your area, recording the precise co-ordinates of each treasure box as they go. The treasure must be hidden very carefully. You can then go off with an adult to find the treasure, using GPS to locate each box from the co-ordinates.

Photo trails Try using fun photography apps outdoors. For example, go out with some friends and take it in turns to send each other photos of things in the park using an app such as Snapchat. Each person will have a quick glimpse of the pictures. Can everyone find the spot each picture is taken from? Who is the fastest to run to the spot where the picture was taken?

Kim's game Test your memory by using an app such as Snapchat to send a series of pictures of things in the park, such as a snail shell, a feather or a chewed leaf. How quickly can your friends find them all. Who remembers the most?

Safety tips Don't hide treasure on private property. Don't damage plants or anything else when hiding or searching for treasure or clues.

tips for staying safe when going wild in the city

Have fun outdoors but please follow these guidelines, which will help you to look after the natural world and stay safe.

Leave no trace
All the activities in this book should be carried out with respect for the natural world.

- Respect all wildlife.
- Be considerate to other users of green spaces.
- Dispose of waste properly and take all litter home with you.
- Take responsibility for your own actions.
- Only collect loose things and plant materials that are common and in abundance.
- Leave wild places as you find them.

General safety guidelines
- Never play in wild places alone.
- Never play in places where there is traffic.
- Always have a first aid kit handy and make sure someone knows how to use it.
- Always take care when playing or exploring near water.
- Only use night lights or candles under adult supervision and never leave lanterns unattended.
- Don't collect poisonous berries or plants.

- Wash your hands after working with wild clay and other natural materials.
- Only use sharp tools such as bradawls, skewers, secateurs and scissors under adult supervision.

index

acknowledgments

Many thanks to all of those who have given us help and advice, in particular Peter Stillwell, Caroline and Anya Carr, Annie Davy and her colleagues at the Barracks Lane Community Garden and Caroline Chapman and her class in Walthamstow in London. Thank you to all the children whose creativity and imaginations have been so inspiring, including Daisy and Monty S; Donncha and Saoirse B; Digby, George and Amelia B; Freddie, Elsa and Maggie G; Laura V; Sebastian and Samuel G; Amy, Annabel and Matilda S; Johnnie F; Megan S and the many other families and friends who have supported us in so many ways. A big thank you to all the children we met at events at East Oxford Community Centre, the Natural History Museum Wildlife Garden in London, Magdalen Wood and the Earth Trust in Oxfordshire and the Hay Festival in Wales.

Many thanks to our husbands, Ben and Peter, and our children, Jake, Dan, Connie, Hannah and Edward, for their support and all the fun outdoor adventures we have shared over the years.

And thanks to everyone at Frances Lincoln.